REACHING OUT
TO OTHERS

REACHING OUT
TO OTHERS

Agnes Bierbaum

Library of Congress Control Number: 2010916580
ISBN: Hardcover   978-1-4568-1144-0
             Softcover   978-1-4568-1143-3
             Ebook   978-1-4568-1145-7

This book was printed in the United States of America.

To order additional copies of this book, contact:
Xlibris Corporation
1-888-795-4274
www.Xlibris.com
Orders@Xlibris.com
84036

CONTENTS

DEDICATION

To the poor, infirm, lonely, elderly, and those who care for them.

Also

To my husband, Gene, for his encouragement and help with the technicalities of putting a book together.

FOREWORD

We can think of no one better qualified
to write a book on reaching out to others
than Agnes Bierbaum. For the past nine
years, Agnes has been deeply immersed
in volunteerism at nursing homes in
Gainesville, Florida. Agnes was one of
the first to volunteer for Friends Across
the Ages, and she has remained a constant
source of inspiration for the new volunteers
who regularly visit the elderly and infirm in
nursing home settings.

From the beginning, Agnes has added
special touches to her volunteer efforts.

Her home-baked treats have become symbolic of her love for the residents. She is affectionately loved by both residents and staff who have named every Tuesday Agnes Day on their weekly calendar of events. She calls every resident by their first name, chats with them, and brightens their day.

In this book, Agnes talks about the many areas of volunteerism awaiting those who wish to give. In addition to volunteering in nursing homes, Agnes has offered her services in soup kitchens and nature centers as well as in church, campus, and community settings.

The reader will draw inspiration from the stories that Agnes tells, and almost everyone will find some kind of volunteerism in which they feel comfortable and have something to contribute. Volunteerism has its own special rewards, and in this book, Agnes opens the door to those who are willing to help.

Steve and Allison Blay
Founders
Friends Across the Ages

INTRODUCTION

In fifty-four years of marriage, my husband and I have moved seventeen times, pursued three advance degrees, raised five children, and taught for over twenty-five years. I mention these accomplishments only to show the busyness of our married life. It was only natural that when it came time for retirement, we knew that we would need to find something to fill our time. It was unlikely that we would find happiness in reading books, watching TV, working on the computer, or just relaxing. We had common interests but also had individual endeavors to pursue. My husband, during his years of teaching, served as a professional parliamentarian for numerous state and national groups. He was interested in continuing this profession in retirement. My interest was volunteerism.

Since my retirement in 1989, I have volunteered in a variety of settings and with all age-groups. In this book, I share some of my experiences in the hope that it may encourage others to find the satisfaction and contentment I have found in reaching out to others.

CHAPTER I

The Forgotten Ones

Very few people can resist the appeal of a small child. Their smile or funny antics immediately draw us to them. A trip to an animal shelter brings enthusiastic exclamations when petting a playful puppy or stroking a furry kitten. A visit to a nursing home does not elicit the same responses. An image of an elderly person in a wheelchair with a twisted body and vacant stare frightens most people. Fear drives us away from interacting with our senior population. This is unfortunate because those who have already lived a full life have so much to give back to us.

For the residents of nursing homes, the days are long and usually uneventful. Sitting in a wheelchair in the hallway watching staff and occasional visitors stream by is about as exciting as it gets on a typical day. In the winter of 2001, I first became interested in a ministry called Friends Across the Ages. The goal of the organization is to seek volunteers to visit and become friends with nursing home residents. My first friend was Willie. She was blind, a severe diabetic, and confined to bed or a wheelchair. I felt apprehensive on my first visit when the activities director commented, "Willie really doesn't talk that much." It took several weeks before we found common interests and experiences and began to talk with ease. She was religious and enjoyed having me read passages from the Bible and sing some old church hymns. Our friendship became stronger, and when she passed away, I was honored to give some reflections on her life at the funeral.

With each visit to the care facility, I met new friends and learned about pieces of their lives. Actually, after Willie died, I did meet my new friend Verlene while she was sitting in a wheelchair in the hallway. We chatted for a short time, and as I got ready to leave, she asked if I would bring her a bag of corn curls the next time I came to the home. After checking to be certain that Verlene could have this snack, I purchased a small bag of this crunchy treat to bring on my next visit, and a friendship that lasted several years was born.

Residents in care facilities are going through a traumatic time in their life. Many are suffering from debilitating health issues and have lost their independence. They are thrust into unfamiliar surroundings and living conditions. The daily support of family and friends is lost. Building new friendships is a difficult task. This is where volunteers need to lend a helping hand.

Small acts of kindness, thoughtfulness, and regular visits convey to nursing home residents that they are still important and someone cares. Greeting cards, calendars, and other small gifts are coveted by the residents as a way to keep track of time and stay in touch with family and friends. A smile, wave, special treats, and a friendly "How are you today?" all encourage a warm friendship between residents and volunteers.

Bingo and crafts can be fun, but residents often prefer to engage in responsible tasks that impart a sense of worth. Several years ago, a few volunteers worked on sprucing up a courtyard area. Bill, one of the residents, took pride in watering young plants from his wheelchair and performing other small garden tasks. Robert, another resident, enjoyed feeding the birds bread crumbs he collected at mealtime. Recently, I complimented a patient on her wonderful smile and how it brought comfort to those who were sad and downcast. She glowed with a look of satisfaction that she was doing something worthwhile.

A volunteer in a nursing home is rewarded in countless ways. The pleasure seen in the faces of residents for the smallest acts of kindness is exhilarating. The fascinating stories these seniors relate will be forever etched in your mind. There is the one my friend Thomas told about killing a skunk, burying it in the ground, and pouring water on the grave to eliminate the terrible odor. After two to three hours, he exhumed the skunk, skinned it, cut it up, and fried it in peanut oil. He swore it was delicious. Another friend, Al, explained how he caught fishing worms, placed them in a pan with onions, and later used them as bait. The smelly onion worms greatly increased his day's catch.

Become a friend of the aged. Possibly, an elderly senior in your neighborhood is experiencing loneliness and would appreciate a visit. Couples with children sometimes make it a family project to visit care centers. If you are not convinced that visiting an elderly patient is meaningful, remember what Mother Teresa said about ministering to others: "We ourselves feel that what we are doing is just a drop in the ocean, but the ocean would be less because of that missing drop."

Agnes with Verlene,
her nursing home friend.

CHAPTER II

The Power Of Music

Music is a gift to be treasured by people of all ages. Listeners and performers experience comfort from simple melodies. Music can soothe, excite, startle, calm, and move us. Stories abound about the healing effect of music.

My husband and I met at college while playing in the orchestra; therefore, it is only natural that our joint volunteer activities focus on music. We use our mountain dulcimers to entertain at nursing homes and retirement villages. While playing at Dudley Farm Historic Park, we engage children in interactive songs. One little girl delighted in displaying her step dancing skills to the tune of

"The Irish Washerwoman" played on the violin and dulcimer.

Another joint volunteer venture with my husband is teaching line dancing at an Alzheimer's day care, assisted living facility, and a rehabilitation center. With the help of staff members and a few residents, a humdrum hour is transformed into a toe-tapping, hand-clapping event. At one facility, an elderly resident in a wheelchair moved her feet rhythmically to a lively tune. After the music stopped, I spoke to the lady about her participation. She was all smiles and said, "Wait until I tell my family I was dancing. I didn't think I would ever dance again." What this lady did may seem insignificant to the observer, but to her, moving her feet to the music was a delightful accomplishment and brought back treasured memories.

Alzheimer's patients with no verbal communication are able to sing the lyrics of familiar songs when accompanied by an instrumentalist. I have found this to be true when singing with a vocal group called the SweetNotes. We sing forties and fifties songs at care facilities. When performing, the audience can be seen and heard singing the lyrics to songs popular sixty years ago, but when we mingle with the residents after the program, many are unable to speak coherently. My mother-in-law suffered from Alzheimer's disease in her later years and lost the ability to communicate verbally. The day before she passed away, however, she sang all the lyrics to "Amazing Grace" when accompanied by a small wooden music box.

You do not have to be an accomplished musician to utilize music in your volunteering. The use of recorded music and group songs can bring satisfaction to many. The lyrics to an old German round aptly describe music as an ageless entity in our lives:

Tho all things perish from under the sky,
Music and Joy shall live never to die.

The SweetNotes,
a volunteer singing group.

CHAPTER III

Nature's Treasures

Having grown up on a farm, tending flower gardens and caring for a variety of animals, I looked for opportunities to volunteer in outdoor settings following retirement. Nature centers attracted my attention.

Lime Hollow Nature Center in upstate New York was my introduction to the joys of nature. Here I led groups of school children through the woods and meadows to learn about wildflowers, pond creatures, trees, and birds. Not only did the children learn, I also gained greater insight into all the beauty around me.

My next stop was Western North Carolina Nature Center in Asheville, North Carolina. Rather than teaching, I worked on clearing trails, caring for the butterfly gardens and general upkeep. While working on a trail, I heard the mournful cry of a young cougar cub. I followed the sound to a fenced enclosure where a small cougar was curled up in a ball pressing against the wire. I carefully reached through the fence, tickled her behind the ears, and she started to purr. Later, I found out that her mother had been killed in the mountains and the cub was brought to the center for care. I promptly named her Val because she was so valiant to survive the mountain ordeal. I wrote a song about Val that I still play on my mountain dulcimer:

Val lived in a cage from a very young age.

She purred every time I came near.

Her eyes were so green and her nature serene.

Now she was sure loved by us all.

Val will never be free to roam from sea unto sea.

All she asks of us now, is to love her when she

does call.

Most recently, I have volunteered at Morningside Nature Center in Gainesville, Florida. For a number of years, I found myself deeply involved in an event called Farm and Forest Festival. I was in charge of the craft tent where children came to make items from natural and recycled materials. More recently, I have played folk tunes on the dulcimer on the front porch of the 1800's log cabin.

The tasks to be performed at a nature center are very diversified as you can tell from the above descriptions. If you enjoy the outdoors, a nature center may be the ideal volunteer setting for you. In this age of global warming and wildlife extinction, a volunteer can help to preserve nature and reach out to others at the same time.

Gene and Agnes
with a group of children
at Morningside Nature Center.

CHAPTER IV

Schools, Community, Church

Anyone who has raised a family has already chalked up many volunteer hours in the schools. My husband and I have served as PTA officers, music club presidents, chaperones for band and orchestra trips, and fund-raising sponsors for the music department. Our children are now grown and raising their own families; however, I have still found opportunities to volunteer in the school setting. My first encounter was with a program called Rockin' Readers. Once a week, I worked individually with those students having difficulty with reading and comprehension. Another school opportunity presented itself at the university level. I interacted conversationally with foreign students.

Many experienced pronunciation problems, comprehending double meanings (e.g., blue/color, blue/sad) and idioms (e.g., raining cats and dogs, over the hill). Since my career field was speech pathology, the Rockin' Readers and foreign student projects were of special interest to me.

Local newspapers are usually filled with requests for volunteers in community activities. While reading a local paper in Cortland, New York, I learned about an organization called FISH (Friends in Service Here). Volunteers were asked to transport individuals to doctor appointments or grocery shopping. Weekly visits were encouraged to the homebound. Local papers also reported a constant need for ushers at community orchestra programs and theatrical productions. You reward both the community and yourself when you volunteer to help out.

One's church affiliation may provide opportunities for volunteerism. Parish members who are hospitalized or living alone require frequent visits. Churches constantly clamor for more choir members and religious education teachers. The demand for food preparation never diminishes. Over the years, I have done all of the above.

At one parish, I helped prepare bag lunches for the homeless. The local shelter did not have kitchen facilities, so the church used their activities center kitchen for food preparation. It was a unique volunteer project. Parish members picked up leftover food from local restaurants, bakeries, and grocery stores and dropped them off at the church. Kitchen volunteers used these supplies to make a bag lunch consisting of a cup of soup, sandwich, fruit, and a doughnut.

One morning, when I arrived at the kitchen, I found I was the only volunteer present. I was panic-stricken. The only thing I knew to do was to start heating water in a large vat and pray that leftover soup would be delivered from a local restaurant. This could be the base, and then I could start adding vegetables from the grocery store and hash browns from fast food restaurants to make a hearty soup. I finally called the director of the homeless shelter and told him I was the only one on duty. Fortunately, he quickly came to my rescue. The soup and bag lunches were ready on time.

As you can surmise from my brief sketches, there is an ongoing need for help in schools, churches, and community events. Look for settings where you feel comfortable volunteering. This will make your involvement fun and rewarding for yourself and for those you are helping.

Agnes with a group of ESL students
(English as a Second Language)
at the University of Florida.

CHAPTER V

Little Things Mean a Lot

There was a love song in the fifties titled, "Little Things Mean a Lot." Part of the lyrics went like this:

> Throw me a kiss from across the room.
> Say I look nice when I'm not.
> A line a day when you're far away.
> Little things mean a lot.

There is a great deal of meaning in these words. The small things we do for each other really do matter.

In previous chapters, I have enumerated a variety of settings where each of us can make a difference in someone's life. Not everyone has the time, health, or mobility to engage in a volunteer activity on a regular basis; however, there are still many small tasks that can be done from home. The Box Tops for Education found on so many food products are collected by many schools to defray expenses. I send mine to St. Joseph's Indian School, Chamberlain, South Dakota, 57326. This same school is also interested in different notions and household items. The metal tabs on drink cans and many other food products are collected by a local Ronald McDonald House that provides housing for families staying in the area while critically ill children are treated at a nearby hospital. A manufacturing company in the area pays a dollar amount for every pound of tabs collected. The Ronald McDonald House reportedly benefits by five to six thousand dollars a year from this collection.

In lieu of collecting items, a phone call or letter to a homebound friend, relative, or neighbor can do so much to brighten an otherwise dreary day. Even the smallest effort may produce a positive impact on someone's life. One of my favorite quotes from Mother Teresa of Calcutta is "We will never know how much just a simple smile will do."

A simple hug means a lot.

CHAPTER VI

Lifestyle Changes

It is not the years
in your life that count
but the life
in your years.

This sign appeared on a billboard fronting a church. Think about it. You could live to be a hundred but fail to make an impact on the lives of others. On the other hand, you could die at a relatively young age but have lived a life filled with compassion, generosity, and sacrifice. This is what will be remembered.

From a very early age, our lives are going through constant changes. Perhaps as we are completing high school, we begin to recognize that there are important decisions to be made. Are we going to college? What career field will we pursue? If we do not go on for higher education, what path should we follow? Once established, we continue our journey through life perhaps with the added responsibility of parenthood and becoming more proficient in our chosen field. Suddenly, before we know it, we are thinking about retirement. Until now, most of us have not thought about what we would do once we were no longer employed. Slowly we become aware that retirement is a new life unto itself.

Recently, I came across a word that was new to my vocabulary. The word was *generativity*. *Merriam Webster Dictionary* gives *generativity* this definition: "A concern for people besides self and family that usually develops during middle age;

especially a need to nurture and guide younger people and contribute to the next generation." To me, this defines what retirement should be. We have now reached a time of our life when every minute of each day is not programmed. What are we going to do with our free time?

Are we going to while away the hours meaninglessly or will we take up some of the responsibilities performed by the retirees before us? There is still a need for volunteer services to the elderly, supervision of young children, countless tasks to be performed in libraries, hospitals, schools, communities, parks, and neighborhoods. Now is the time to make a decision. Hopefully, it will be a wise one that gives you satisfaction and enjoyment and makes a difference in the lives of others.

Gene and Agnes playing the mountain dulcimer
at Dudley Farms Historic Park.

www.ingramcontent.com/pod-product-compliance
Lightning Source LLC
Chambersburg PA
CBHW050347290526
45785CB00006B/2673